We Go to Town

Written by Lynette Evans
Illustrated by Daniel Lloyd

We can all go to town.
Can we go in the bus?

4

The bikes go to town.
We all go on foot.

The taxis go to town.
We all go on foot.

12

We can go to the top!
WOOOOSH!

GETTING STARTED

Activating prior knowledge: Ask students if they have ever gone to town with family or friends. Ask them how they got there and what they saw.

Encouraging prediction: Using the interactive digital book, or the printed version, read the book's title to students and have them discuss the characters on the cover. Turn to and read the title page. Ask students to look at the illustrations as you move through the book, identifying characters, different vehicles, and settings. Have them use the illustrations to predict what the story might be about.

Outlining focuses: Explain to students that as well as finding out about the family's journey to town, they will talk about capital letters at the start of a sentence, and words with a short *u* sound.

DURING THE READING SESSION

■ Literacy

Modelling: Read the text to students. Use expression, pause to clarify unfamiliar words, and point to details in the illustrations, such as the car's flat tyres on page 3.

Guiding: Invite students to read, keeping in mind what was modelled. Use the specific abilities and needs of the group as an indication of when to assist by pausing and giving prompts or clues. Suggest strategies, such as using picture cues and knowledge of letter/sound patterns.

Interacting, interpreting, analysing, and evaluating: At appropriate intervals and/or the conclusion of reading, ensure students are making meaning from the text by asking what has happened to the car, bus, and train, and why the family has to go on foot. Explain that the family must live close to the city. Ask what the family does when they get to town. Remind students of the difference between imaginary and informative texts, and ask which they think this book is.

■ Literature

Literature and context: Ask students if the author of this book has told a story that is similar to their own experience.

Responding and examining: Ask students how they felt when they saw the car, bus, and train could not be used. Ask them to use the illustrations to tell how the characters' moods changed during the story.

■ Language

Expressing and developing ideas: Ask students how the illustrations on pages 2 to 7 helped them understand the problems the family has getting to town.

Text structure and organisation: If you are using the digital version of the text, explain to students how it works. Remind students that a capital letter is always used at the start of a sentence. Ask them to look at page 2 and tell you two words that start with a capital letter (*we*, *can*).

Sound and letter knowledge: Revise upper and lowercase letters by choosing some from the text, printing them on flashcards, and having students sort them into two piles.

Discuss the sound of the short *u* in *bus* on page 4. Ask students to think of words that start with the short *u* sound, then sound them out. Write these words on the board. Have students circle the short *u* in each. Ask them to list short *u* words in rhyming pairs (for example, *up*, *cup*; *tug*, *mug*).

PUTTING THE LEARNING INTO PRACTICE

Small group/independent activities: Have students reread the text independently, then proceed to the activities listed in the Teacher Guide.

AC

Springboard

Connect

MACMILLAN

ISBN 978-1-4586-3972-1

9 781458 639721